The

TWENTY

Things you need to ~~learn~~ learn in order to find the ~~love~~ love of your life.

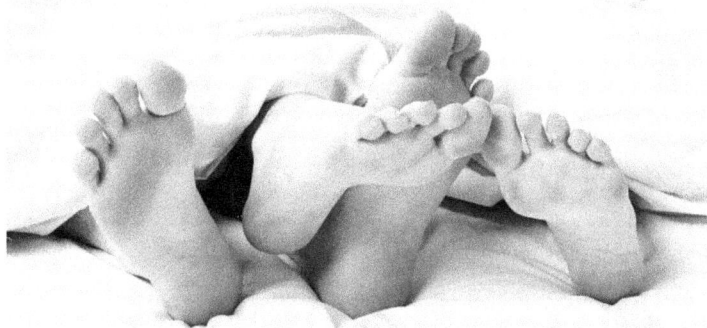

STEVE SAPATO

Published by For All The Marbles
www.stevesapato.com
www.facebook.com/stevesapato

Design and layout by Mullins Creative, Inc.
www.mullinscreative.com

ISBN 978-0-9830557-0-9

We are each of us angels with only one wing. And we can only fly embracing each other.

~ Luciano De Crescenzo

DEDICATION

This book is dedicated to my family: Arcie, Dorothy, and Cheryl who started it all, and to Zach and Erin who have allowed me to love them.

It is also dedicated to two amazing ladies who showed me what love really is and to a few wonderful people who have recently come into my life to help me put this book together and through the processes I have needed to learn. It is their loving touches that brought my dream to fruition.

And to Dr. Leo F. Buscaglia, for without his vision of love, none of this would have happened.

I love you all!

~ Steve

FOREWARD

This book could have been called *Love Is Not Enough*, because that is the truth of life, isn't it?

Let's face it, we have all been in love with someone who we knew was not the right person for us … cried, agonized, worried, cried, argued, fought, cried, broke up, got back together, cried, broke up … and in the middle of it all, we knew we loved that person but we also knew it was not going to ever work out no matter how much we wanted it to. Love is not enough.

If what you are wanting is someone to love … first learn what love is. The greatest problem in a relationship is the lack of understanding love. *What is love? How do we share it? What committment does it take to make a lifetime of love last?*

It is amazing to me that we spend hours, weeks and months studying a subject such as trigonometry or calculus or years learning how to do a job and to be better at our hobbies and yet, we almost never study the most important aspect and foremost desire of our lives … love.

That is what this book is all about. So, if you are ready for some doses of reality, ready to stop hurting about a relationship and ready to start a path of wonder, romance and finding the right person for you … and ready to change … you have the right book in your hands.

TABLE *of* CONTENTS

INTRODUCTION

The purpose of this book is to help you clarify if the next person you are attracted to could be the love of your life.

Let's start with some easy questions:

1. What is a great relationship?
Can you answer that? Before you go any further, please write down what you think makes a great relationship.

_____

_____

_____

_____

_____

_____

_____

_____

_____

_____

_____

It is important for you to answer this question because it is the knowledge of yourself that first needs to be clear.

2. What makes a great partner?

Now write down your answer to this question.

_____

_____

_____

_____

_____

_____

_____

_____

_____

_____

_____

To read further without answering the questions implies that I have insight into your psyche and that I know who you are and what you want. I don't. Everything we will discuss revolves around your knowledge of yourself or the lack of it. Do you know yourself? Please stop and take a few moments to answer those two questions, it's critically important.

There are two separate questions for a reason. Relationships are not people and people are not relationships. They are separate and should be treated separately. So take the time to seriously think about these questions and answer them as if your future depends on them. It does.

Do you believe you truly wrote down what you think is a great relationship and what you think makes a great partner? Are you locked into what you want? And what you don't want? If so, then let's begin.

Dr. Laura Schlesinger cites in her book, *The Proper Care And Feeding Of A Marriage* a *Time* magazine article from 1993, "early love is when you love the way the other person makes you feel" while mature love is "when you love the person for who he or she is."

When we "fall in love" we usually fall with our hearts and nothing more. It is that initial attraction that brings us together. And quite often it is that initial attraction that keeps us feeling a certain way and leads us to making a commitment to a relationship.

Think about the last time you fell in love and then fell out of love. *Why did you fall in love? And what made you fall out of love?*

Again, take out your pen and write down the things that made you fall in love with your last partner.

_____

_____

_____

_____

_____

_____

_____

_____

_____

_____

_____

_____

I am on *Facebook* and work with numerous groups and personalities. One person recently asked the question, "What is chemistry and how important is it to a relationship?'

There were dozens of responses and most of them said chemistry was vital to a successful relationship. And several tried to describe chemistry.

The consensus was that chemistry is the feeling that comes when two people are in harmony and this harmony affects the emotions of the parties involved. This affect can be in the comfort level of each person, making conversation and interest a smooth operation instead of a struggle in the process of learning about one another. Chemistry makes it easier to relax and enjoy the moment, it eases body posture and enhances the sense of humor.

Chemistry can be felt by one or by both people.

But there is more. We need to know if the person with whom there is chemistry matches up to us on other levels as well. We are not just romantic people. We are psychological and we are physical as well.

While it is through romance we typically select our partners, it should be much more than that. We watch movies, read books and hear songs that all tell us that if our hearts pound, our bodies sweat and their kisses have fireworks, that person must be the right one.

But, we have many emotional sides … issues and areas that we need fulfilled. Likewise we have many other levels—intellectual, physical, spiritual—all of which have various levels within them as well. Unless these needs are met and satisfied on many levels, our relationships are not going to bring us the satisfaction that we so desire … long lasting, wonderful and fulfilling.

So let's start with the chemistry of the emotional level.

CHAPTER 1

Oh! Look What I Found!

Have you ever heard someone say, "I always seem to pick the wrong kind of person?"

Have you ever said it? Do you know why that is?

I have had dozens of people say that to me over the years. And I always come back with the same response? "Really? Why do you think that is?" And their response is usually ... "Gee, I don't really know."

Of course I ask the next question in this tale of success ... "Well, what are you really looking for?"

And do you know what most people say? You probably guessed it ... they almost always say, "I don't know."

So question number one is, "Do you know what you are really looking for in your next significant other?"

The reason this book was written was to help you find your last significant other; to help you find your "soul mate" to help you find "true" love, the kind of love you want, are willing to share and most importantly willing to "accept."

How do you find the one you have been looking for if you don't really know what you are looking for?

Have you ever heard of someone finding a coin that is worth millions of dollars? Do you think that person just stooped over and picked up a random coin, took it to a coin collector and the collector said, "Congratulations! You are a millionaire!"

Or have you ever heard of someone discovering a painting worth millions of dollars? Do you think they just pulled a painting out from a closet and the art expert standing by said, "Wow! You are so lucky! That painting is worth a million dollars!"

Probably not. The coin they "discovered" is one they knew was rare because they had studied, researched and investigated coins. They knew about coins because they had a genuine interest in them. You and I have picked up coins off the ground hundreds of times in our lifetime and never even glanced at the stamping. Even if we would have looked we would have seen nothing important because we didn't know what to look for.

Looking at a painting is exactly the same. You and I could have pulled a dozen Manets, Monets or Picassos out of the storage room and never known they were worth millions because we didn't know what we were looking at.

What if every time we found a penny we ran to the coin collector? Every time we found a painting we called the art collector? I suspect that if we did that, very quickly, the art connoisseur would start charging us for his opinion ... for his evaluation of each and every painting. Eventually we would be spending great sums of money just to find out if that painting was worth anything.

But isn't that what you have been doing with your dating life? Spending great resources, huge amounts of time, money and emotion just to find out if the person was even worthy of a date? And then, because we are human, we are affected by our own beliefs, feelings, and pheromones.

We get that chemistry running and wow is she gorgeous! Wow! Is he handsome! Wow does he have a great car ... great body ... great ...

Do you see that the love we see on TV and the movies is all about emotion? And while we want that wonderful passionate emotional feeling, we need to understand that love, lasting-a-lifetime, soul-mate love is about much, much more.

You may not have realized this but you may have treated your selection of partners with the same callousness with which you would have picked up that random coin. "Oh, look what I found, I think I will keep it." Or, maybe just the opposite. We are the coin! Oh, look who just found us and picked us up. I think I want to be kept! And from there, we start a relationship that will use all of our resources, time, effort and energy when we didn't do our homework to see if the relationship was worth keeping.

Let's talk about the difference between love and infatuation.

CHAPTER 2

What Are The Odds?

It is widely known that half of all marriages end in divorce. By age 30, three-quarters of the women in the U.S. have been married and half cohabitate outside of marriage. (CDC-series report 23, #22. 103pp) and there is a 20 percent chance that a first marriage will end in divorce within five years while the probability of a cohabitation ending within that same time frame is 49 percent! After ten years, the probability of a marriage ending is 33 percent while cohabiters face a staggering 62 percent. Gary Chapman writes in his book, *The Five Love Languages* that within 15 years the divorce rate will be 43 percent for married couples.

Do these numbers amaze you? And if they do, why? How much time have you spent studying how to be a great partner? How to show love? How to give love? How to accept love? What to look for in a partner?

The fact is if we never study, we can't expect our knowledge to help us succeed.

So, why do we have such a staggering failure rate for relationships?

I have several theories on this. The first is that cohabiters start off not willing to make the marriage commitment because they are afraid of failure. (If you disagree because you know couples who don't marry for many reasons, that is OK, too. I am simply making a presumption for couples that have no true reason not to marry.) They start off with a failure mentality and are unwilling to commit completely because of their own innate fears! They fear it and they bring it to fruition.

But why are they so fearful? Because of the statistics. I have heard people say things like, "Well, we are probably not going to make it anyway so why make it so hard to split up!" or "Why get married? I don't need that kind of commitment this late in life."

What is the response to fear? The standard line is, "fear creates a fight or flight response." We prepare ourselves for the inevitable. And as our relationship emerges, good and bad traits appear. And from our preparation we are ready for what comes and we deliver what we prepared for.

Have you heard the jokes that end in ... "and then the fight started"? Or have you heard about the men "going to their caves." Have you ever wondered why women are perceived as naggers and men as bad listeners? We instill in our psyche the images of defeat.

My second theory of why cohabiters are more likely to end a relationship rather than live happily ever after is the societal concept of living together.

Living together typically does not bring the same emotional commitment level. It has a "convenient" arrangement that can end at any time and both parties understand that. No matter which partner moves in with the other, one will always have an advantage. I have heard this said, "This is my place and you can leave whenever you want!" or "You know, this isn't my place and I can walk away whenever I want!"

Cohabitation simply does not convey the same determined tenacity that is required of a marriage.

Yes, I do know there are many examples of successful live-in relationships, but we are talking here about the norm, the predominant, not the exception.

Someone recently told me that she would never marry again unless there was a prenuptial agreement. You need to know this person has been divorced for 25 years. And probably lots of good reasons why. A prenuptial agreement is merely telling a future potential partner that when we split up, they can't have any of our stuff.

A prenuptial agreement is not the basis of a grand and forever marriage. I know and I understand the reasons for a prenuptial agreement. I have heard the arguments on both sides every single time it comes up in a discussion. And I will never understand it. If I love someone enough to live with them, either through marriage or just a consensual agreement I should trust them enough to share my whole life with them.

A prenuptial is merely the "living together" status when thinking you are actually getting married. One person will always have an advantage in this situation. Well, go ahead and leave, you aren't getting any of my stuff!

The statistics do prove that marriage is longer lasting than cohabitation. And this brings us to a place where we need to talk about what love really is.

CHAPTER 3

What Is Love?

When we talk about love, we have to understand there are all kinds of love, aren't there? The experts offer six types of love: Eros, Ludus, Storge, Pragma, Mania and Agape. We will talk about them ... just not by those names. We will use more familiar terms when we talk about the types of love, what love is and what love isn't.

Think about the types of love. There is how you love your your mom and dad. You love your sister or brother different from them. You love your pet different from them. You love your friends in a different way again. You love, love, love, love, everything differently!

And it is also true that you love someone differently at different times in a relationship. You might have loved your husband or wife madly and passionately in the beginning and then … it became a quiet, demure, warm kind of feeling. If you are reading this, however, you are most likely single and hoping to find a forever, new love.

The good news is, you don't have to stop loving one person in order to find a new love of your life. You might still love a past partner but now it has evolved into a different kind of love.

Love comes in many forms. One of them is infatuation. We call this many different names. One of them is puppy love.

If you have children you have probably witnessed it, or if you have spoken with young people about love you may have found yourself tempering your conversation with your own thoughts. But when the young folks walked away, the comment may have been made that they were just experiencing puppy love! They will get over it.

Do you know that puppy love can cause great pain? Do you know that teenagers suffer the highest rate of suicide from the emotional disaster of a broken or failed relationship that some may have dismissed as just puppy love?

Puppy love is infatuation and that is the most passionate kind of love. It can be wonderful and it can be disastrous! Infatuation brings out the best and the worst in people and can cause us to do an assortment of things from climbing mountains, writing poetry and singing songs to stalking someone and outright crime, abuse and even murder!

Infatuation makes people do crazy things when unchecked or misunderstood.

Here we will be talking about the good kind of infatuation love. Love is controlled. It can be wild! Passionate! Unfailing! Unimaginable! Which sounds like infatuation but the difference is, in a typical dating relationship we think of infatuation as being short lived.

When we are typically infatuated it is usually more chemical and romantic than is it loving, generous, kind, giving and understanding. Infatuation is demanding, controlling and jealous driven. Infatuation is love but it is more like love on steroids. One never knows when it is going to go wrong.

Infatuation is selfish and ego driven. Infatuation is all about self.

Infatuation typically takes us through the first stages of a relationship but when it comes time to settle down and make commitments about giving, sharing and understanding, then infatuation begins to fall apart for it is none of those things.

Love on the other hand is all about your partner. When you fall in love it should be a wonderful, amazing and fulfilling. It should make you happy and seldom unhappy.

Before we continue with infatuation, let's talk a little about happiness because there are people who seem happiest when they are unhappy, or have something they can complain about. Those are the people who are constantly complaining. Even when everything is going good, these folks find something to upset the euphoria of the moment, day or week. These people will be part of our equation on loving people but they will always be the exception.

For many people, unhappiness is more a part of them than happiness. Unhappy people can fall in love. When they do, they show the very best part of themselves. They put their best foot forward. Therein lays one of the many potholes of relationship shopping. We'll talk more about the potholes of a relationship in later chapters when we discuss the need to know your partner.

Infatuation is all about what one person can get out of relationship. It is the "I" of relationship drama. What I need, what I want. Once the other partner discovers this selfishness, the relationship may come to an end. Discovering that the other person places their needs, wants and desires over ours causes us to miss something in our relationships and we start pushing them away or distancing ourselves.

Infatuation relationships are short lived in comparison to a much greater and loving relationship.

There is also the love that develops out of a friendship. As friends, you might work together, or have friends you share or you might have been involved in an activity together and the relationship started out as going with the "gang" to eat or drink and the relationship became something more.

Many times this kind of love is longer lasting than infatuation love but much less passionate and typically just as unfulfilling after a similar period of time. It is a shared emotion, entertaining and comfortable but many times does not lead to the marriage kind of relationship. This is because in a friendship love situation, the friendship is based upon specific behavior in order to blossom and grow.

If you are bowling partners or volleyball teammates and the activity subsides for the season, you may find you have much less in common and even fewer reasons to get together. The relationship may last for a while but if another activity takes its place and you both do not share that activity, the distance between you grows. The other person will spend less time with you and more time participating in the new activity.

Likewise, working-together love or "office relationships" develop because we share similar interests. These are more likely to develop and last since the interest typically continues. However, if a promotion or lay-off happens, the relationship changes and often times, one partner will step back as different interests of the job or new job develop.

One of the greatest challenges of a relationship is for both parties to show interest in their partner's daily activities that they themselves are not directly involved in. Will your partner be willing to listen to your stories of the daily grind and all the things that you might want to share when you get home?

Another type of love is one I like to refer to as ... *I Love You*. This love makes people want to make a commitment. It is the love when someone might say "I love you" with the hope that the words would be returned. If they are returned, the process worked and if they aren't, the process didn't work.

I Love You love is the most simple of our love emotions. This is the love that we share easily from the time we are adolescents and it is the innocent and patient kind of love.

We look into one another's eyes, looking for the signs, looking for that forlorn eye contact that says, please say it. Please tell me. And when the moment is right, we offer that wonderful innocent kiss and then whisper it to our partner, I love you.

Love itself is the most amazing gift we can offer another person.

If you have not read *The Five Love Languages* by Gary Chapman, I would recommend it ... I would demand it of you before you move on to your next relationship. We will utilize many of the theories and concepts discussed in that book and elaborate on how knowing yourself and your partner are going to be keys to a successful search for your next significant other.

Knowing yourself is going to be THE KEY to finding someone who you will be able to spend the rest of your life with. Knowing yourself will become a wonderful, passionate unfailing part of you so that you understand how the chemical makeup of love and simply the right chemistry will make you fall in love ... but by knowing yourself you can recognize and move beyond mere chemistry to a more lasting, fulfilling and permanent relationship that will be all you have ever dreamed about.

CHAPTER 4

The Ultimate Goal

How are you going to find something when you don't know what you are looking for?

That question was posed to me many years ago. It made sense then and it makes sense now. I recently posted a couple questions on Facebook, asking how people find new partners, and how they will select their next partner. The answers did not surprise me.

Here are some of the responses:

- *I will know them when I see them.*
- *I will let my heart decide.*
- *I will let God choose my next partner.*

But when I suggested they plan for their next relationship I got the standard response, "If I have to work that hard at it then I don't want it," and "Planning is for vacations!"

Yes! Someone got it! Planning is for vacations …
planning is for many, many things!

And why do we plan? So we can succeed! So we can
have a good time and so we can reduce worry.

A plan is often called a goal. Goal setting has such
a bad rap when actually we use it every day. When
you go to the grocery store and take a list, you have
planned – when you buy off your list you are achieving
the goal you set for yourself. We use lists and plans in
every aspect of our lives.

Ask a sales person if they have goal, every single
one of them will say, "yes." If they are serious about
success, they may have goals on how many phone calls
they will make, how many people they will see, how
much money they will make, how many sales they will
make, or how many deals they will close. They will
tell you that without specific goals in mind they would
not succeed. Talk to successful people and they will all
share that they set specific, achievable goals in their
lives, even though some will seem unattainable or
unrealistic to many people.

So why don't we plan for our next significant other?
Why don't we put together our list of goals for whom
we want, what we want and why we want them?

I know a man who had recently divorced and as he
tells the story, he was sitting watching TV one night
and wished his next wife would be a little exotic and in
his wants he asked for her to be able to speak a foreign

language. He wrote it on his goals list and put it away. Five years later he rediscovered that notebook and was happy to discover that he had been married for three years and his wife spoke two languages. Coincidence? Maybe, but what if it wasn't ...?

So let's do a little goal setting so we see the importance of setting our goals for what we want to accomplish in our lives.

We'll start with these four rules.

Goal-Setting Rules

1. Write down your goals
2. Put your written list in places where you can see it every day
3. Share copies of your goals with people who will help you achieve them
4. Change your goals as you change.

The first rule makes our goals more concrete. Putting them in places where we can always see our goals will increase our chances of having them come to fruition. Sharing our goals gives us support. The last rule is important to understand because goals are not written in stone and never to be altered. Goals are the written intentions of your desires, wants and dreams and they will change as you change.

When you were young, you most likely had different desires than you do today. When you were young you might have dreamed of being a firefighter or a doctor.

Maybe you have achieved those dreams. But if you were to choose a job at age 60, you probably would not choose either of these professions due to the physical requirements or the years of education required. Your goals would be different. When you were young perhaps you wanted a Ferrari two-seater sports car but now you are older, you know that just getting out of a car that low could be a challenge. The same holds true with your love life. A few years ago, maybe the quality you desired in your significant other you don't really care about today.

Your goals and dreams change as you change and that is not only OK, it is necessary. Update your goals list as often as you need to in order to reflect your current desires.

Here's an example of how a goal may be updated due to the passage of time. When I was 25, I wanted a 20-year old with a perfect body and long hair, but now that I am 60, I can see that the perfect body is only what I want to see, and has very little bearing on reality. The long hair is seldom found on an older woman and most wear short or mid-length hairstyles. So long hair may be an unrealistic goal.

Another example of a goal change might be that you specified a trait you would like in your next mate. Then you date someone who provides that trait and you find out it wasn't nearly as important as you thought it was. Therefore, your list could change after you stop dating that person.

Or your list may need clarification. You may have put on your list that your ideal someone must "talk to me, share with me and be a talker" because your previous partner never shared or talked. And then you meet someone who is a talker and at first you are thrilled and thinking, "Yes, I finally met someone who will talk!" But after a few weeks you discover talking was all they wanted to do, talk, talk, talk, talk, talk! Now you are thinking, "Don't you ever shut up and just listen?"

You said talker. You wrote talker. But you meant communicate!

So remember as you grow, as you learn, as you come to different understandings … your list will change and you will find your goals will change along with your desires.

CHAPTER 5

As The Caterpillar Asked In Alice in Wonderland, *"A-who, arrrrre a-you?"*

When you think of the last person you fell in love with, do you remember the beginning as wild? Passionate? Amazing?

The same thing is true of your next significant other! The feeling will be wonderful! The emotion, amazing. The passion, incredible!

And ... you might be looking right at the love of our life right now ... or not. But how do you know? What don't you know? And how do you know what you don't know?

This journey is to help you discover exactly the kind of person you are looking for.

But first, let's talk about you.

Who are you?

As you search for the perfect mate, what do you think makes you the perfect mate? As I talk to people, one of the strangest things I hear are these words … "They should love me just as I am." I say strange because most of us are constantly changing, evolving, moving to become something that most of us will never even figure out even as we become that person. And yet, some of us will never change. What a shame that is!

The Twenty
The truth starts with you.

This process started for me more than 20 years ago as I had heart-felt conversations with many people, conversations that included discussions about past relationships. We would all share about past partners, what we liked about them and what we didn't like about them. Many times we fell into discussions about hidden topics that are seldom, if ever, talked about. These were our deepest, darkest most secret areas of desire and distain. Some may be considered taboo in some circles.

So when I say we talked about our deepest, darkest most secret areas many times we talked and shared about sexual things. But we also talked about even more private things … our desires, the things we wished that our next partner would have, would do or would offer.

Maybe you have had these experiences like this.

Maybe you have shared these discussions. And maybe you know someone like our friend Beth, who dated someone for more than two years. She fell in love, shared her life and passions and after two years married the man of her dreams. She divorced less than six months later because her new, wonderful husband suddenly changed and started physically abusing her right after they got married.

How can this be? How could someone hide such behavior for so long and maybe more importantly, why was Beth unable to discern or discover such behavioral traits in more than two years of dating and sharing her life with this man? What could possibly happen that would allow such behavior and such undiscovered traits?

After several questions I was finally able to stumble upon a "red flag" that should have been a warning sign but it had been totally ignored. Why was it ignored? Because Beth was "in love"! And we all know that when we are "in love" it's easy to ignore signs and signals unless they are thrust upon us.

In Beth's case, her future father-in-law had made one simple statement. He said, "If my son ever does anything to hurt you, tell me." When she said he had told her that, I asked, "What did he tell you when you asked him what he meant by that statement?" Beth said, "I never asked him about it."

And this, like so many other things we do or don't do, could have helped her immensely in making the final decision to marry or not. But since she was "in love" she was not looking for reasons, signs or indications that he was anything but perfect for her.

And in that is the inherent challenge of allowing your heart to decide who you will or will not spend your life with. We stop looking for any indications except the ones we want to hear.

When we find someone we "click" with, or who is our soul mate, or who is so wonderful, our emotions take over and control our lives, we hear what we want to hear. We feel things because it is so right. We stop listening even if someone, a good friend, a relative, tells us things that should make us question our own feelings or this relationship. We want to be in love! And it's a great feeling!

Don't misunderstand, I am not necessarily saying you will marry this person or commit your life like Beth did, but how do you discern who is right or wrong for you? Have you ever chosen the wrong person? Some of us have chosen the wrong person many times over. And over and over and over.

Even more importantly, how much do you find out about someone to be sure that someone is right for you? How much time are you going to spend with someone if you already know they are not going to be the one you are going to choose?

One of the purposes of this book is to help you decide how much time you will give to someone, how much effort you will spend if you know within a couple meetings that this person is not the one you seek.

Fate

I asked the following question in a small survey I conducted, "If you have the opportunity to find the love of your life, what would you do to find a person who made you happier, who loved you more than you have ever been loved before, who made you yearn to be with them and who you missed terribly whenever they were gone. And, how will you know when you find them?"

Here are some of the answers.

"Steve, I am just coming off finding someone who I thought fit the bill until he acknowledged he '... isn't ready for a relationship.' and I just '... got away on him' for a year! I'm not doing well but realize, I need a new system! Do you have one?"

"I found him when I wasn't looking ... when I was content with me ... when I was happy and when I didn't need anyone to complete me but to compliment me."

"We need to be content with ourselves, not looking, and then it will happen!"

All of the above are true because people can find the right person when they are content with themselves. But many times they find them after spending considerable time around the other person's friends.

They had learned about the person before actually meeting them.

Another person said:

> *"Positive thinking is the key, about yourself, your life, the person you want to find. Negative thinking will kill everything but positive thinking can change all aspects of your life for the better and things will just fall into place naturally."*

Have you ever heard that? Have you ever said that? Is this how you used to think? I say used to think because you are reading this book. If you are reading this, then something must not have worked like you'd hoped it would.

Zig Ziglar said, "Positive thinking can't do anything but it will allow you to do everything better than negative thinking can!"

Most of us have never studied love. We have seldom, if ever, read books on love. Hardly ever attended a seminar on love. We think love will simply "happen" because it is such a natural thing.

The truth is, love as we believe it to be, does not exist. Wait! Qualify! I need to qualify all 100 percent comments. 100 percent comments are when I say always, never or does not exist. As well as many other statements. We all know someone who has fallen in love, and shares that love with the perfect individual for them.

Those people are blessed. How can it be so simple for them when so many other people struggle and struggle and struggle. I do think they are blessed, because for so many other people, finding the love of their life seems to be an almost impossible task.

Love is not about fate. It is not about getting lucky. It is not about God putting the right person, the perfect someone, in your life. A few people have found their prince charming or Cinderella in their first partner but the rest of us have to invest the time to find that perfect someone. The rest of us have to kiss a lot of frogs to find our prince or princess.

And remember the frog that you reject today could be the prince for someone else tomorrow. So always treat those frogs with respect and dignity.

The truth

If you are divorced or failed (people are funny about their beliefs and what they will admit to so always allow and cover all the bases) or ended a relationship, have you ever analyzed what went wrong?

Without blaming anyone, can you figure out what went wrong in your past relationship(s)? Have you ever just asked yourself, "What could I have done to make this relationship work?"

For most of us we certainly have tried. But it is so hard to analyze. The truth for most of us is, the relationship ended because one of the partners decided that it should end. Maybe they didn't tell you or you didn't tell them that in so many words but through actions it was decided that the relationship would end.

Someone cheated on someone, someone lied to someone, someone got bored with someone, someone didn't share enough with someone, someone didn't give enough, love enough ... or maybe someone gave too much? Gave too many hugs, touched too much, kissed too much, wanted sex too much. Someone just ruined it.

For whatever reason the relationship stopped working.

If you have read *The Five Love Languages* you might have already discovered many reasons your relationship did not work.

If you know and understand your own needs, your own love languages, your own heart's desires then you might also understand what was missing in your last relationship.

At the time of this writing, I am single. People ask me all the time, "If you know so much why aren't you married?"

My response is this. *The Twenty* is designed not so much to find the love of your life as much as it is to help eliminate those who are not going to be the love of your life. In that endeavor, *The Twenty* is designed to help find that one special person who you will most likely be able to create a lifetime of joy, love and lasting love.

So, to ANSWER THE QUESTION! I have found that by knowing exactly what I am looking for, by using the skills and methods I have described, I have been able to narrow down who I am even willing to go out with and do not take precious resources, energies and time go out with people who are not right for me.

I have found I am much happier, much more satisfied and less frustrated because I don't have to go through the love/hate situation that accompanies so many dating stories. I don't get too deeply involved and I make sure as we talk, the people I am sharing with also understand how my relationship search works so they can utilize it also.

So you can see, I am not married because I know exactly who I am looking for but have not found her yet. The process is working.

And in this journey don't be afraid to sift through a lot of people. Don't be afraid of rejection and rejecting. Don't be afraid to meet all kinds of people because you are looking for only a couple who will be able to meet your standards for what you truly want in your life and who you want to share your life with.

We are looking for that one-in-a-million!

Finding love would be great but what does love mean to you? It means all kinds of things to different people.

What have you learned from your past relationships? What do you see as the giant problems in a relationship? What is the falling apart process?

What kind of person are you looking for? There are so many people who are out of whack. So many people on medication ... so many people who suffer from depression.

I went through a phase in my life when I said, "I think I am ready for some anti-depression medication." A very good friend asked me if I was serious. I said I was, and she replied that we could get some from some of our friends! I asked her what she was talking about and then she started to list all of our mutual acquaintances who were on medications.

I was stunned! Most of the people I knew were on some type of medication. Most of these people were well off and in some kind of relationship. Families. Jobs.

What in the world would make them so depressed that they would have to take medication? What can't they handle by themselves? How bad could their lives be?

Our society is over medicated!

I was talking with a beautiful lady recently. She is an aerobics instructor with a great full-time job and considerable responsibility. From the outside, she appears to have it all together. She proceeded to share with me that three years prior, she and her husband had gone to counseling and in the first five minutes the counselor said, "You are suffering from depression aren't you?" She said, "No." The doctor said she had all the classic symptoms and before the session ended was prescribed with medication to treat her illness. Three years and one divorce later she is still on that medication. And it came from an immediate diagnosis from someone who had spent a very short time with her!

Could the doctor really know her that well in such a short period of time? If you have no clue you are depressed, wouldn't you at least question the need for medication?

So, how quickly can we know someone? What could they be hiding from us? And why?

It is our job to find out. People are not always truthful. That is one of the great keys to your successful search for the right person for you.

So let's get started with the things that will help you find that one great love of your life that will last forever.

Let's start out with some basics.

First of all ... no one is to blame for your last relationship. Relationships happen and unhappen. They begin and they end. Some for reasons we understand or relate to and sometimes for no rhyme or reason at all.

After reading this book as well as other books on loving relationships you can never blame another when a relationship ends.

Having an affair is devastating to most marriages but it's only a symptom of a bad relationship ... something is lacking in one or both of you.

I heard a woman recently tell an on-air radio personality that she believed her husband was at least talking and sharing intimate things with another woman if not having an actual physical affair. The radio therapist asked, "What is that woman giving your husband that you are not?"

The lady responded with, "I gave him a child!" A child is a wonderful gift but does not replace the love and affection that we all need to share in our personal relationship.

And when pressed she finally offered that the other lady was giving him affection, attention and sex! And the therapist asked ... "Are you having sex with your husband?" She said they hadn't had sex in more than a year!

Now I am not saying that sex is the glue that holds a relationship together but that is part of a loving and gratifying intimate relationship.

How good, how satisfying is your relationship? What kind of relationship are you offering? Have you invited your partner to share what they are wanting? Needing? Hoping for?

The Twenty is a bare-essentials look at what you really want in your next significant other. They can include things you don't want, too.

In putting together a list of 20 things you want in your next significant other you are putting down things that you know will make you happier if they have them. These things must, however, be freely offered and given by your significant other to make you happy.

This list evolves from finding the real you. If you recognize what makes you happy then you can begin to look for something in another person that can enhance or feed that need.

An example of an item on this list might be that you will not date or marry or choose for your partner anyone who smokes. This is actually too mundane to put on your list. It is actually something that without even saying it, without even writing it down you know you will not accept. So I don't recommend it unless you have not decided that behavior is totally out of your choosing.

Further explaining that ... if you write down that you want someone who doesn't smoke but if you really love the person and if they meet your other goals you might accept a smoker, then put that down on your list because it is something you will accept. If on the other hand you already know, that there is no question at all, that you will not even think of dating a smoker, then you needn't put it down ... you won't date a person who smokes and therefore you won't have to worry about whether that behavior is on the list.

You only want to put specific things on your list that would constitute in your eyes a great relationship.

We are going to delve into many areas that you may have not even thought about or certainly didn't think was important until now.

As you to begin to create your list, you will want to think of all the qualities you would want your perfect partner to possess. And as you write this list you will discover things about yourself. There will be things you discover that your new partner must have and things they must not have.

When you are doing this, keep in mind that the more specific your must-have list is or the more specific your must-not-have list is, the harder it will be to find that person who fits into your list and into your life.

Here is an example. I know ladies who wrote on their list, *"If a man is not making at least a six-figure income, I won't date him."*

They have dramatically reduced the number of eligible men. Bear in mind that according to government statistics, only 18 percent of all employed people earn over $100,000 annually. So if this is truly one of the criteria, then they are looking for only 18 percent of the entire population. Let's assume that most of those making this income are male (yes, I know, I am sexist!) And that leaves approximately 10 percent. I don't have the statistics for how many of that 10 percent are single or available, so let's just guess that leaves 5 percent of the entire population of the United States. That's all they get to choose from, five out of every 100 men they meet. Now how many of those five are attractive to them physically, emotionally, intellectually, etc. and you see they have a huge task in front of them.

We do have to keep in mind that all of our desires will reduce the number of available people and remember that we are only looking for our one-in-a-million partner.

Some people date incessantly. Some are constantly on the dating sites. Some love dating. Some hate dating. The social networking sites of today are wonderful and amazing. They offer companionship, they offer entertainment, they offer communication and they offer insights! Another advantage of social networking sites is that you get to invite and ask all kinds of questions to help you decide if you even want to meet.

You can find out so many answers before you ever meet face to face! Because of all of the social networking you can use email, phone, Skype, text messaging and many more tools to ask questions before you ever begin to invest your time and heart into a relationship that was never meant to be.

So the first step in finding the love of your life ... *learn to listen.*

The twenty – how do you decide?

How do you decide what you truly want? How do you know? Our greatest challenge is in knowing what we want. How will you decide? How many times have you asked the question, "What do I really want?" If you are like most of us, the answer to that is seldom.

Goal setting is basically what this is all about. If I asked you to write down 100 things you really want to have, do, be or become before you die most of us couldn't write down 20. We never think about it. We never plan on it.

Twenty things you want before you die? Seems almost too easy but here is what we do … we judge. We filter. We limit everything by what we have already experienced or by what we have come to expect. We decide based upon what we are, what we have done and what we have failed at in our lives.

When I ask people to write down 100 things that they want to achieve in their lives most people cannot do it. They stop themselves. When I ask, do you want a Porsche … a Mustang … a Ferrari … most people will say, no! But if I had asked them that same question when they were 17 years old? Almost all of them would have given a positive answer or provided their own dream car or house. When I ask people in their 40s and 50s if they want to travel, most say, not really. But when I ask my classes of freshmen college students, almost all say, yes!

So what has changed from the time we were teenagers with all of these dreams until today? Reality! The real world has changed and so have our expectations. We have created our own limitations by what we have experienced and now we limit ourselves in order to not be disappointed.

I once heard a story about a trained flea circus. It was all about a tiny little tabletop event where this person had fleas in all sorts of jars and containers and not once did those fleas jump out of their habitat. Some fleas jumped eighteen inches to the top of a container while others only would jump two inches to the top of their own container. Miraculous! People were amazed!

But you see, the trick was simply that each flea was kept in a closed container and would jump and bang into the top trying desperately to escape time after time until one day they just stopped trying. And in knowing that if they jumped too high they would bang into the lid they finally developed a muscle system that allowed them to jump but never reach the top and therefore never bang into that lid again. So once trained the owner could take the lid off and none of the fleas would ever escape.

We have trained ourselves that way. Many of us have tried things and failed. Many of us have experienced things and failed. Many of us have hoped for things and never had them materialize. So, we change our expectations so that we will not experience failure ever again.

We stop at where we think our limitations are and never try any harder. We don't want to be disappointed again.

We treat our love lives like that as well.

Do you know that there are three kinds of attention?

1. Good Attention
2. Bad Attention
3. No Attention at All

Most people don't even think about the third kind of attention. But it is the reason people put up with abuse. It is the reason children go back to abusive parents and the reason wives or husbands stay with abusive spouses. People would rather be treated badly than ignored. And it's true for almost all of us, even those of us who won't admit it.

So how does this relate to finding the love of your life? *We have to break all barriers!*

How many of us want another divorce in our lives? How many of us are willing to go through another breakup?

What are you doing today to reduce or eliminate going through all of that ever again? What new knowledge are you learning? What new ideas are you learning? Are you the same person you were during your last relationship? Are you looking for the same things? Do you know what you are looking for?

Did you know that most relationships fail, not because of one huge problem, but because we allow all of the little problems to manifest into a huge problem.

When I peruse profiles I find very few like this, but keep in mind this was a response to my question:

Thank you for taking the time to read my profile and for the lovely compliment. What am I looking for in a mate? I think most people know what they do not want but have more difficulty describing what they seek (I don't believe I struggle alone).

I know that the person I seek will have a well defined sense of humor. He will be educated but able to relate to many types of people and will be curious about the world around him. He will be compassionate toward others in need and will probably be actively involved in community service. Since I manage my finances well, I will expect the same of him; I believe it is difficult to begin a life partnership when one is always giving while the other only takes.

On a different note, I do not believe he will be handsome in the classic sense. I would more likely be drawn to his imperfections, such as crooked teeth or a rather large nose. I have always found myself drawn to a craggy, interesting face rather than one of perfect symmetry. I suppose there is something devilish about me; I rather like the fact that I can find beauty in the faces of men that others might overlook.

I will also admit that I would expect passion. Here I am, a true southern woman, trained from childhood to suppress physical needs, yet I simply do not care. Could there really be anything finer than to lie naked in the arms of a man who truly understands passion?

Some may question why I have remained unmarried for most of my life; if I know the qualities I seek, it should be an easy search. Unfortunately, I think most failed relationships occur because people choose incompatible partners. They normally do this for two primary reasons; impatience (they want immediate gratification before doing the work of truly getting to know the other's character) and they are unrealistic in their perceptions (if he really loves me he will change). I differ in both respects because I rather enjoy the journey of getting to know the other person and do not feel pressured to "meet mr. Right." I suspect that it will happen when, and if, it is the right time to do so. I also am interested in a man's true character and simply have no desire to change anyone. I believe that there is a significant difference between "compromising" and "settling" and am unlikely to "settle" for just anyone at this juncture in my life. My mother always said, "you can tell the character of a man by how he treats his mother and animals." she may have been slightly biased, I'll admit, but I have found a lot of truth in her adage:)

*I do not know if you will find any of this useful
in your research. I suspect that you did not
expect this lengthy response; you may even find
that you do not agree or like any of the things I
have written. Please understand that these are
only my perceptions and thoughts and they are
probably not shared by others. I do not know if
another self-help book is the key to unlocking the
mysteries of the heart but I wish you well in your
endeavor. Since you have admitted that you are
also single, surely you understand my skepticism
regarding your ability to help others find the
"love of their life"? I will certainly be interested
in seeing the final result. At least you have one
interested buyer already:)*

Do you think this woman has insight into what she
wants? Maybe. And do you think if she reads this
book she will remember writing it? Maybe not. And
do you think she has all of the traits she spoke about
written down on a list that she can refer back to?

CHAPTER 6

The List

Oe of the greatest challenges we face in deciding who we will choose as our next significant other is that it is a choice. *A choice.*

Some people will never find another partner because they are afraid of failure. They hurt so much from previous relationships that even thinking of starting a new one scares them to death. We all know people who will always be single because they will never allow themselves to make that kind of mistake again. They never date or have a prolonged relationship in any manner.

You need to know that your next significant other is your choice.

And to truly understand it is your choice, is to understand yourself. This book is all about learning about you: your needs, your desires, your wants and your wishes.

If you are familiar with Wayne Dyer, Gary Chapman or numerous other motivational authors then you know or at least begin to understand that your happiness starts with you. Your happiness begins with you knowing, allowing and accepting yourself. Once you know yourself, once you accept yourself, for all that you are, your strengths and your shortcomings, your faults and your weaknesses, then you can begin to look for something in others.

Do you know your own shortcomings? How can I ask for someone with patience and understanding when I am sarcastic and critical of them? How can I ask for someone who doesn't hold a grudge or get angry when I do nothing but push all the buttons that makes him or her upset or angry?

If we know ourselves then we can change ourselves or at least learn about ourselves well enough to be able to help explain ourselves to our partners. We can then help them understand and accept us and in so doing, learn to accept them.

What causes most relationships to fail is a lack of understanding between two people. It doesn't have to be discord or arguments, it can simply be a withdrawing from one another. If we start our relationships passionate and romantic and then one of us fails to maintain those feelings then the other will withdraw, looking for what we gave them originally.

Understanding ourselves enough to know how or why we have "changed" can certainly keep things in perspective.

I hear so many people upset with their partners because of something someone did or didn't do. I call this "should have" miscommunication. When you leave a hint or give them a hint you are asking for disappointment. Take the time to share and explain exactly what you want.

Have you ever heard someone say, "They should have known ... what I meant ... what I wanted ... what I was feeling ...what they were supposed to do." Nope. No one should have understood anything if you didn't explain it right.

Many times our own expectations ruin our lives.

A very successful friend of mine, Burt Gulick, shared a philosophy that I think should rest with every couple. That philosophy is simple—*What would you expect if you were single?*

If you are single, you do everything for yourself. So why does it change when you find a partner? And why does it become an argument or create hard feelings when your significant other doesn't do what you expect them to?

His philosophy was if his wife or he were to ask one another to do something they refused, no matter the reason, they could not get upset with each another.

If you are standing in the garage unloading groceries and you call out for your partner to help and they don't … do you get upset? Why? If you were single you would unload the groceries all by yourself. If you argue with your partner enough about it that you divorce and you find yourself single, who will help you with groceries then?

I know. Some of you are thinking right now, if that lazy so-and-so wouldn't help me bring in the groceries I would rather be single … then know that about yourself and maybe stay single. Or maybe you could change to where you would allow that type of behavior and life would be good? Remember it could work both ways. No, not to get even, but if you didn't feel like doing something some time, they would not get upset with you either! How glorious would that be?

So in reading this maybe you are learning about yourself? Do you think you know yourself well enough to start that list?

Get out your pencil and paper and start writing down anything that comes to your mind about what you want in your next significant other. One of the keys to this list is to not judge yourself for what you want. It is OK to be "picky" here. It is your list and no one else's. It is ok to be discriminating. Rude. Selfish. Harsh. It is OK because this list is *all about you*.

Perhaps you could start with physical features. Do you want your new love to have dark hair? Long hair?

Curly hair? Big lips? Little lips? Narrow eyes? Round eyes?

I know what you are thinking... looks aren't that important. But to some people, they are.

So describe what you want your next partner to look like. Don't worry, the list will be narrowed down from possibly 100 to a few things. Do you want a 34" waist? A 22" waist? Large hips? Narrow hips? Lots of hair? No hair? Facial hair? Wears fragrance? Doesn't wear fragrance?

Now let's do the same thing for the emotional and mental part for your next partner but you will find this to be much harder.

An example of this might be ... *I want them to love me.* But what is love? What does "love me" really mean? It's much more than, just to love me and to tell me they love me. But those are certainly parts of showing love.

So, your first few might be something like ... *they tell me they love me every single day without me having to ask ... they show me love every morning by waking me with a kiss ... by saying, "I love you and I am so lucky to have you in my life."*

Or it might be ... *they show me they love me by being in the same room with me: when I do the laundry... when I watch my favorite TV show ... when I read a book.*

What does love mean to you and how will it be expressed to you by your next partner in an ideal world?

Love isn't a simple thing to show or receive. When you think of feeling loved what do you think of? What makes you feel loved? Is it words? Actions? When you dream the impossible dream what fills your mind and makes you feel so loved you could crumble into their arms and be safe and secure?

See, love isn't simple or easy. It is complex and overwhelming. It is not what you see in the movies until you find that person who makes you feel like the characters feel in the movies!

So, write down what you are feeling and thinking now. Don't limit yourself. Dream! Dream it all right now! And write it down.

I know what you are probably thinking ... *no one will ever be all that I am imagining right now.* You might be right ... but what if you are wrong? What if you were to write down all that you are wanting right now, what if they were only most of that? Would you be unhappy if they were 90 percent of what you are wishing for right now?

This list is merely the beginning process. So don't be afraid to write down everything now, it can be narrowed down later. Write down everything you wish and hope for.

If you wrote, *"must be a hugger"* ... what does hugging

mean to you? Do you want a quick hug when your significant other leaves for work and you are satisfied until the next hug when they go to work again tomorrow? Write down specifically what you want.

I know people who have said their significant other must be a good kisser and in counseling they complain about the kissing. Not that their partner is not a good kisser but it's the duration of the kisses ... the timing of the kisses. One client of mine included in her list that in her next significant other she wanted to be kissed while they make love. She said her ex was a great kisser but never kissed while they were making love and she longed to be kissed during their lovemaking.

Many ladies write on their lists that they want their next partner to cuddle, hug, kiss and talk after making love and for their partner to not to just roll over and go to sleep. They want to be romanced afterwards.

I know both men and women who included in their lists that they wanted their partner to stay in bed after they made love. Rushing to the bathroom made them feel cheap and dirty.

These are simple things, that are easy to ask for and easy to do by a significant other who wants to make their partner happy.

So, emotionally, are you writing down what you want?

I want someone who will stand beside me when I fail no matter the outcome. I want someone who isn't jealous. I want someone who will feel comfortable at parties when I just wander and meet new people and I don't want to worry about their jealousy. I want ...

Write it down. What do you want?

So, stop reading and take some time to write.

How did you do? How many things did you write down?

If you are like most of us, you are probably still judging yourself and limiting your list based on by what you have already experienced in your life.

OK, here's another method for accomplishing this.

What is your favorite romantic movie? What makes it romantic? What do you like about the relationships in that movie? What would you like your relationship to be like considering that movie?

Now go write again, please.

OK, still need help?

Think of the best relationship you know. Do you have a friend or acquaintance that seems to have the perfect relationship? Why does it seem so perfect? What do you see that makes it perfect? Write down those things if you envy that couple. Write down the things you see in them that you would like to have.

And as long as you are at it, write down the things you see in other couples that you would refuse to accept in your relationship. There are good things but there are also bad things that we would refuse to have in our relationships.

And sadly, if you have ever had an affair, what made that other person seem so wonderful. Write down those things. Because when the relationship started it was wonderful. But usually the things that made it wonderful faded causing your relationship to end. Or maybe they only faded for your partner and you are still wondering why it ended.

CHAPTER 7

The Nitty Gritty And The Itty Bitty

Now let's take all of the things you wrote down and refine them. Let's get to the nitty gritty and find out what you really want.

You should have at least 30-40 things you want in your next significant other. Some of you will have 50-100. And that is good. Let's see if we can help you refine your list so that you truly narrow down what you are looking for in your next partner. We'll pull it apart and analyze it.

We used one example earlier, the hug. If you put down something like, must like to hug, we need to clarify what you meant. Did you mean a person who hugs you one time when they head off to work? Did you mean they must want to hug you when they come home, every night when you are sitting on the couch watching TV? What kind of hugging do you want?

A brother or sister hug? A friend hug? There are all kinds of hugs!

This is also true of love. Some people write down "they must love me." What do you mean by love? Do you mean make love? If that is true, how often? In what manner? What things do you want in a lover and partner? Did you mean emotional love and what manner of love shows love? Do you mean you want them to kiss you every morning? Wake up and tell you they love you? Call you every day? Text you hourly? What exactly does "want them to love me" mean to you? Show physical love? Adore you and write you poetry love? Put up billboards professing their love? Remember your anniversary love? Hold your hand? Smell your hair? Cook with you? Do laundry with you? Massage you? What means love to you?

What you need to do, for each item on your list, is to look at all of them one at a time and be explicit in your clarification of what you want.

I want my next partner to be exotic and speak a different language. Does that mean speaking in tongues like in the Bible? How about if they spoke American Sign? I know, it sounds ridiculous, but I am trying to help you establish what each and every one of your "wants" really means to you.

I want someone who takes care of me. What does that mean? You want someone big and strong? Financially rich? Sends you money? Makes love to you twice a day? What do you mean, "takes care of you"?

I had someone tell me she wanted their next hubby to be strong, that she was tired of wimpy men. Wimpy in manners, wimpy in looks, wimpy in behavior. She wanted someone who would stand up to her, sometimes tell her no, not always "give in."

Seven years later she was divorcing her dream guy. *Why?*

The things she thought she wanted, she didn't want at all. Her strong man wouldn't let her go shopping. Wouldn't let her get her tattoos. Wouldn't let her go on trips with her girlfriends. He kept tight rein on her financially and didn't let her buy the things she was accustomed to buying. He was strong but he was also jealous. And while she thought she wanted a man with a little jealousy to step into her "limelight" and be this handsome powerful guy who would make her feel good, when he stepped between her and guys who would flirt with her, she found he scared those other guys away and she needed their attention to feel good about herself.

She ended up with someone very similar to the first husband who she divorced thinking she wanted someone stronger.

Do you know what you want? Have you written it down?

Recently a woman sent me her list. On that list was: family oriented, funny, ambitious, loyal and affectionate. She wanted my feedback and direction based on the four top things on her list.

Here is my response.

First, read ... no exception ... read *The Five Love Languages* this week! ASAP. This is one area you will need to know in order to find him/her.

Now let's work on terminology. What exactly do you mean by family oriented? Is family oriented that they take on all the responsibilities of being a family person? Taking the kids to soccer practice? Watching all the games? Going shopping for groceries? Shopping with the family for clothing needs? Or do you mean, coming home and sitting with the family around the table for dinner? Staying home and watching TV? What does family oriented mean to you?

What do you mean by ambitious? I recently met a woman who wanted her man ambitious and when he was offered a job for big money he left her behind to pursue wealth. Do you think that was what she meant? Or do you think she meant ... *sheesh...just have a freakin' job!*

What exactly is loyal? You mean your partner doesn't fool around? You mean your partner stands up for you when someone says something negative? You mean when the tough times happen he stays with you, understands and helps you through it? Or do you mean he will simply stand beside you at events, always be close to keep you company, always attend things you want to attend? What do you mean ... *loyal?*

What is affectionate? What makes someone affectionate? Constantly touching you, sniffing your fragrance, rubbing your butt as he walks by you, brushing his hand against yours at every opportunity? Or is that excessive affection to you? When you say affectionate does that mean he holds your hand when you are out in public? Kiss you lightly before you go to bed and say "I love you." What is affection? What affection means to some would drive others crazy! Affection to some is needy to others. Affection to some people is almost no attention to others. See what I mean? It's all up to interpretation ... and we need to know your interpretation of these terms.

You are going to find several sub areas in your list. It is a given that there are the "must-have" and "must-not-have" parts of your list that you cannot and will not compromise.

Some people put must not use hard drugs but that is a daily given and you have probably lived by that for years now. You won't even consider someone who uses these drugs. Don't put that on your list because you have already decided in your whole person that you won't be with someone who uses hard drugs.

But what about other areas? What have you written down that are areas of compromise?

I know some people whose list is 100 items long. The chances of finding someone who will meet all 100 are zero! (Yes, I know as soon as I wrote zero someone out in book land has met and married and is living happily ever after with the person who met all 100 items on their list. But again, the chances are miniscule, OK? Here's what I am saying … you just got cut from my list! I want someone who will not pick me apart for such little things.)

Did you get that one? Someone that nitpicky is probably not someone I want to spend my life with. Nitpicky, and my definition of what makes someone nitpicky, will now be on my list. Notice I said "probably" in that previous paragraph. While I would want someone who would accept my foibles and not correct me most of the time I might accept them as my partner if they met most of the rest of my list.

Must Have and Must Not Have

As we reduce this list down we will put things into must-have and must-not-have sub-groups.

They must be thin. They must smile a lot. They must laugh at my jokes even when they have heard them 100 times. Are all of these true? Are they must-haves? Nope. You might accept someone who, by some standards is not thin … suddenly you find yourself completely attracted to someone chubby. And you need to know, share and talk about this with your potential partner if and when you get that far along in your relationship. Remember we talked about when to broach some issues in your relationship? First dates are not the time to say something like, "You know, you are heavier than the people I usually date but for some reason you look good to me."

Deal Breakers

But look at your list now, some of the things you wrote down are must and some are must not. These I call deal breakers. You need to know about them right from the start of your relationship.

Those are the areas where you will need to ask the right questions, listen for the right answers, and dig for the information from friends, family and relatives to begin your own personal discernment of those issues.

I have known people who put their list together and wrote very specific things but then found that some of the items didn't necessarily match. One man put "great butt and legs" and then found that the lady he dated had great "butt and legs" but her stomach and breasts were not. He was surprised by his own ability to accept those differences, since he knew his own personal limitations on what he was looking for physically from his partner. He began to understand himself and what he was really looking for when he put on his list, "great butt and legs" that he wasn't really looking for just those as much as he wanted a physical person who really turned him on in her appearance. Since then he has learned that the "package" physically could be completely different and still be exciting to him. "Great butt and legs" are still on his list but now he understands what that really means.

As you look at your list and separate out the must haves and the must not haves you will begin to discern what is truly important to you and begin to learn how you will find a partner who will offer you the things you need in order to more "safely" fall in love.

Give this list to your closest friends and confidants. Explain the list to them and then when you introduce possible significant others to your friends or confidants they will be able to help you discern if these people are right for you because they will hold you accountable to the items on your list.

Your best friend may say, "Wow! At first meeting this person looks perfect for you!" Or, "What are you doing? This person is not the person you described on your list! Run away! Run away now!"

And while you might have the emotional feeling, the chemistry for this person you will be aware that you are walking on thin ice, unsafe territory, or down the wrong path. You might date this person but you are less likely to fall completely in love. You will understand from your list that you can still have a relationship but it is not the relationship you want to consider as the love of your life.

This list is not designed to keep you from dating and having fun, but more to help you discern who might be the person to let yourself fall in love with.

Can anyone match up to everything on your list? Probably not.

But it is important to keep your list manageable. That is why this book is titled The Twenty. It is your responsibility to narrow your list down to the 20 most important factors you are looking for.

Keeping 100s or 1,000s of things on your list will make it almost impossible for someone to match up for you. Reducing your list to those things that you can't live without or the things you can't live with, will bring your true desires to the front and help you decide more easily who might become the love of your life.

Those friends and confidents who have your list will look at you at times and tell you not to settle. But settling is truly what this list has been about. What they mean by settling is to settle for someone who is not "right" for you. But if you find someone on your list that meets most of your list, and you get to decide what "most" means, then you also get to decide who and what you are searching for.

If you have your list of 20 and you meet someone who meets ten of your list, are they right for you? That is not for me to decide, So you have to ask yourself this, "Why did I write down these 20 and how important is each and every one of them to me?"

I have told my best friend many times ... to "settle" for someone who meets 15 of my 20 is not settling for someone as much as it has been a refining down process to see what truly is important to me in order to love someone for the rest of my life.

CHAPTER 8

The Truth Be With You

Know your partner.

I hear this all the time … "But he/she did this for me when we first got together. What caused the change?"

If you were to write to me on AOL you would write to qlman@aol.com. I got that nickname from my students when I taught college. I preached and preached to them, not to believe the things they heard, read and saw until they knew the truth. Q = question and L = listen. Hence … qlman@aol.com.

Did you know that 67 percent of all statistics are made up?

Of course you didn't know that because I just made it up! And that was what I tried to teach my students. Just because I tell you something does not mean it's the truth. Just because someone wrote something down does not mean it's the truth either. And most importantly, just because you read it does not mean it's the truth! What is my truth is not necessarily your truth.

It's what children of the '60s came to understand. The government would lie. The police weren't always your friend. Your friends didn't always tell the truth. The world wasn't Leave It To Beaver, the world was now Dallas.

Have you ever looked at something and said it was blue or yellow and someone else thought it was green?

When I heard this story, it changed my perspective forever.

> *I was sitting across my dining room table talking to a friend once. Glanced out my window and said, "Isn't that a beautiful cardinal!"*

> *He looked and responded, what cardinal. I smiled my knowing smile and said the one right there sitting on the fence. He turned his head this way and that and said, what cardinal, there's no bird out there. I, of course in my wisdom, got smart-alecky and said, duh! That bright red cardinal, right there! Duh!*

> *And he said again, I don't see any bird. Losing my cool for this poor moron of a friend, I finally stood up walked over where he was sitting,*

*squatted to his level, threw my arm out so I
could point to the bird and make him look
ridiculous... and oh my goodness, from his
point of view, the tip of a tree obscured the bird
no matter what angle I moved to ... From his
point of view there was no bird. And suddenly
I realized, we all have a different point of view
about almost everything, even when we are
sitting together and supposedly experiencing the
exact same moment in time.*

So, your truth is not necessarily their truth. Never
assume it is. Always ask.

A woman I was chatting with said her courtship
lasted three years and her marriage only two. When
I asked her why she said, "We found our lives were
headed in different directions. I wanted a life filled
with travel, excitement and helping people with my
gifts and talents. He wanted to retire on the family
ranch to relax and go four-wheeling." When I asked,
"Didn't you two talk about what you wanted from
life in the three years you were dating?" She said,
"No, we were in love and just thought everything was
going to work out."

We assume things are going to work out. Have they
so far? So maybe we should all take a step back and
evaluate where we are in our lives.

I ask myself all the time, why aren't we better?

I ask it in schooling. When I was a teacher, I had many foreign students pass through my door. All of them could speak at least three languages. Were these well-educated rich kids from Europe or China? No, they were from "third world" countries. But they could all come to our country and survive by speaking our language. Yet, none of the American kids I taught could speak any other language well enough to be dropped off in another country and survive. Yes, there is something wrong with our education system but even more ... we don't take on the responsibility to get better.

I recently heard there are online government sites where we can improve our language skills. FREE sites to help us get better. First of all, no one seems to know these sites exist. We aren't seeking them out to grow in our skills either. We think that what we have been taught should be good enough. We think that we do enough already to "get by" in that language. We see no reason to get better, after all, we speak English and anyone coming here should speak English, too!

We do exactly the same thing when it is time to be educated about relationships. We are born with the knowledge to make a marriage work. We are loving creatures so love should just work. We shouldn't have to work so hard to make a marriage work. It should be easy!

Why aren't we better? We don't see a need to get better.

But, if you are reading this, you probably see that need. You understand we all need to grow and learn and improve, especially when it's time to find a partner we are going to spend our lives with.

So let's stop assuming our relationships are going to work out and start figuring out exactly what it will take to ensure they do!

Here is your next challenge.

Let's start to learn to ask questions of our partners before we fall in love. Let's learn to listen to the answers, not just what their words say, and how they might say it, but what they don't say.

A friend once shared an experience he had when his girlfriend's son was getting engaged. Her son was not rich and right after the engagement the man found a copy of the jeweler's bill and was stunned by the cost of the rings. No way could this young man afford to spend that much money, so he asked his partner how this could be. He said the conversation was curious. He asked her how the son could have paid this. She said she didn't know. Hmm, red flag. You might be asking, "Why is it any of his business." That is a good point. The boy spending too much on his engagement and wedding rings should not be his concern but ... we are learning here, that everything affects everything and you should not only ask, but be allowed to ask almost anything if you are in a relationship that is open and trusting and going someplace.

The man then asked, "Where do you think your son got the money?" "Don't know," was her reply. Hmmm, red flag again. His mother didn't know? And she didn't ask him? Not like her. She was always into everyone's business in the family.

So he asked, "Did you give him the money." "Nope," she said. He asked again because her answer was not ringing quite true. Her response was the same, "Nope." Again, there was something not quite right ... Where did he get that kind of money? The man knew the son's credit wouldn't support such a purchase.

Have you ever had those feelings in a relationship? I always call them the warning bells and you should listen if yours go off! The man did and the conversation with his partner went some thing like this ...

The man asked, "You didn't give him the money?"
Nope.

"But he somehow got the money."
I guess.

Hmmm ... different thought process, different tack on the thoughts.

So he said got it now ... "OK, you didn't give him any money, right?"
Right.

"But somehow he got enough money to buy this?"
Yes.

"The jewelry store didn't loan him any money? He didn't finance it?"
Nope.

"But the jewelry store got enough money so he could buy it?"
Yes.

"Ah! So, did you give the jewelry store the money?"
Yes.

"So you did give your son that money to get the rings!"
No.

He said she never did admit that she gave her son any money. But she did give the jewelry store the money. And that was the "truth." How she avoided or saw her truth was a matter of conversation. It was something he dealt with quite often. Finding out the truth by hearing what was not being said, by discerning that the "truth" was only her version of the truth. You may also find this in relationships.

You have to hear, with your inner voice, the truth that makes sense to you. Never believe what you are being told until you verify what the truth is.

The example used earlier is the father saying, "If he hurts you, let me know," and Beth didn't question the statement at all. She was closed off to bad behavior and the thought he was even capable of bad things ... she was "in love."

So when you start a relationship, listen to what isn't

said when you ask a question.

Ask why their last relationship ended. And listen for what is not being said. Well, it was just not meant to work out ... we were different people ... he/she just suddenly changed ... they just stopped seeing me ... I just decided it wasn't working.

Ask probing questions.

How do they get along with their children, her children, his children? Do they talk about liking children? Or is their some other reason the children were a challenge? And then listen carefully to the answers!

Listen for what is not being said.

How often do you see your parents? Do you have a dog? Cat? Pet? And why did you get the pet? I have had people tell me they have a pet and they got the pet because the poor thing needed a home. Nope. They probably got a pet because they needed love.

When we talk about what isn't being said, I ask people why they don't ask. They typically say, "I don't want to seem like I am prying." Prying? This could be your life! Of course you should pry! Ask, ask, and ask again. This is now your job. Your responsibility. It is who you must become to discern the most important things about this person. If they take offense, get upset or refuse to answer, this is probably not the right person for you.

Of course, there is timing in all of this. First dates are not the time to ask about bank accounts, sexual preferences or many other things, but it is the time to ask about their background, family history and criminal records.

I know married couples where the wife is not allowed to ask about the bills or the money. I know widowed women who, because they were never allowed to ask, ended up with huge financial problems when their partners died and left them in a financial mess. You are allowed to ask anything and to get answers or this person is not right for you. I teach women to become powerful because they are powerful. My seminars work on bringing ladies from the timid and servant stage of life into the powerful, yet service, part of life. It is vital that we all understand what it takes to make a relationship work for a lifetime.

How you ask is very important, also. Don't ask like you are a private investigator or a cop on TV! Aggressive questioning will only bring rejection.

I hear about people talking to people but never really hearing what they say. Never really listening. Now is the time to listen, to be quizzical, to begin a true investigation. Not through an investigation company but through your own personal interrogation. Simply ask a question until you get the response that satisfies you. If the answer does not satisfy you, that might be your red flag. Never let a red flag go by without asking clarifying questions.

Please don't misunderstand what I am saying here. Investigating when you are starting up a new relationship is not the same thing as snooping after you are in a relationship. Never, ever snoop your partner. Confront, ask, and discern, but if you trust them enough to live with them don't snoop, follow, listen in, pry, or check-up on your partner. If you have those kinds of doubts then you might think about ending your relationship. Your happiness is based upon trust and without that trust you will never be happy.

As Dr. Laura is known for saying, "Give your partner a reason not to go anyplace else and they probably won't!" I agree.

But if someone says to you, "Wow, I have never done this or I have never felt this way... with anyone else," the red flag should go up. Why? It's not that you are not special but it is that this might not be who they really are. If they have never bought someone flowers or sent them candy or been this affectionate, then maybe they are being this way with you to win your heart and maybe after a period of time they will revert back to who they really are. That special treatment will stop.

I cannot tell you how many times I have heard something similar to this, "But in the beginning of our relationship he did this and this and this. Why did he stop?" It's because he did it unknowingly trying to win your love and affection and once settled into the relationship they will revert back to who they really are. When this happens people experience a loss of intimacy, in the sense that when people first become close they feel a tremendous sense of validation from each other, like their partner is the only other person on earth who sees things as they do. That feeling sometimes fades, and when it does, it can take a heavy toll on the marriage or relationship.

> *Social science has a name for that fading dynamic—"disillusionment": lovers initially put their best foot forward, ignoring each other's—and the relationship's—shortcomings. But after they tie the knot, hidden aspects of their personalities emerge, and idealized images give way to more realistic ones. This can lead to disappointment, loss of love and, ultimately, distress and divorce.* ~ Aviva Patz

So how can you tell? Ask. Ask why they are doing it now? Ask why they didn't do it for anyone else before this? Ask, ask, ask.

And now that we might have a better determination on what you need to find out about your new "date," now you also have to start listening to their friends and relatives.

When you are all out together, what do their friends share with you? What do they share about your date? Some people will make jokes but most jokes about personality and habits are based upon fact.

If several of their friends say something like, "I would never have pictured him/her with you," ask why? And listen.

If someone says something that does not completely answer your question, ask again for further clarification. And in this beginning stage, don't believe a word someone says. Oh I mean believe it but carry your doubts right there on your sleeve. And listen carefully for any sign that their truth is not truth.

Listen for their comments about all topics. If you hear something on TV about an abuse case watch how they react. Cheating spouses? Watch how they react. It's all about honing your skills as a good listener and then qualifying any information you come across.

CHAPTER 9

Your Greatest Challenge

That brings us to a place where most people will stop reading or stop doing what it will take to discover the love of their life.

The greatest challenge you will face is changing you.

You need to change much of what you do because who you are and where you find yourself is based upon your past and all you have done. And where you will find yourself in the years to come will be determined by one thing ... your grasp upon your reality.

If you are reading this then you probably believe your reality is something that needs to change. What's the definition of insanity? Insanity is doing the same thing over and over again and expecting different results. Isn't that what you have been doing for your whole life? You have been doing the same thing to find a date, a partner, a lover, a spouse over and over and you have been ending up in the same situation – single or unhappy or maybe both.

It's time to change. And you will change your current reality by opening yourself up to new ideas and new ways of doing things.

Some of you are still reading this but you refused to write down any of the things you have been asked to. Why? You are unwilling to change. You are going through the motions of wanting something different but are unwilling to be different. Unless you become someone different than you were before you started reading this book, then you will probably keep getting the same results you have been getting.

You have to face your greatest challenge, changing you.

Only by changing you enough to do the small things we have spoken of in this book will you change enough of your life to find the love of your life and perhaps live happily ever after.

So let's make sure of one thing ... do you have a willingness to change?

If you answered yes to that, then stop! Make sure you wrote down all that was asked of you. If not, go back and do it now! No games. No lies to yourself. No procrastination.

CHAPTER 10

The New You

Do you now believe that you can find the person of your dreams? Are you willing to end a relationship that you discover is not right for you? Are you willing to learn about someone before you get involved?

Sex is a wonderful thing but sex brings an emotional commitment much of the time. I know, the men are saying, "no" and the women are say "sometimes." But truthfully, how many times has sex in the first few dates worked out so that you developed a long-lasting relationship with that person.

Especially for women, sex leads to an emotional commitment that is hard to get past. It is much harder for them to back up and start "Questioning & Listening"!

Understand yourself. Understand your limiting behaviors and beliefs. Understand your shortcomings. Understand your strengths and how those will affect others. Understand what others have seen in you and how that has affected each relationship. Understand that people will fall for someone based upon numerous preconceptions. You need to know what leads people to falling for you so that you don't hurt them if you decide not to get involved with them.

The first step to a great relationship is friendship. What is friendship? Think about your true friends. I'm not talking about acquaintance friends. True friends are the ones who will take a day off work to help you move. All the rest are not true friends. So, ask yourself this, what makes someone a real friend to you.

And, what makes friendship last? Why do friendships end?

A real friend stays your friend even when they move away. Other friends fade if we change jobs, stop playing volleyball or bowling. Some friends fade if we go to different bars or clubs. Some friends are rooted in where we are and not who we are.

That simply means you will have friends who you work with but once you change jobs they fade quickly from the friends list. No one's fault but they were your friend because you worked there together.

That holds true for many friends. That will hold true for your significant others. Sometimes we find ourselves drawn to someone by who they are at work or play. We are drawn to their image, their aura, their persona. Take them out of their environment and we don't find them as attractive.

I have shared with people and many times they tell me, they fell for them because everyone at work thought they were gorgeous and wonderful. But when they got to know them, they weren't what they appeared to be at work.

Many ladies fall for the "bad boy" image or the "Harley guy" because of their own emotional imagining for such a person. And then when their marriage falls apart five years later they can't even grasp why.

I have read profile after profile on the dating sites that list all the things a lady wants ... love, romance, someone to share with, someone to hold, someone to laugh with and someone to cry with. To me those things indicate an emotional being ... and then they add ... oh, and having a Harley would be great!

Now don't get me wrong, but many Harley riders ride solo. The guys like to be seen on Harleys because they are macho, they bring attention, they are the bad boy symbol. Sexy, hard, masculine ... aarrggh! They are the pirates of today's society ... the Errol Flyns, the Johnny Depps ... the bad boys.

And ladies love them! But, the bike itself, the lifestyle ... when you analyze what they epitomize ... does it truly fit into your lifestyle? Your perception?

Many true Harley riders ride in cold weather, hot weather, they go on weekends to Harley events. Riding a Harley is like owning a boat, it must become a mistress and it takes up a lot of your time.

Recently several celebrities have ended their marriages because their spouses were caught cheating. Pardon my naivety but if the person I fall for is tattooed and famous for playing around, what in the world makes me think my marrying them will change them? If you marry a bad boy or a bad girl they will probably be faithful for a while because … it is what they are supposed to do, but then they will probably revert back to who they truly are!

There are only three things that will get someone to change … the books they read, the CDs or things they listen to and the people they associate with.

If your partner wants to change but is unwilling to do these three things … bet your bottom dollar they will not truly change to become the person you want and need them to be. If your partner smokes and they say they will quit but they run around with smokers, the odds are against them ever quitting. If they say they will stop drinking but they still hang out at bars, or around friends who drink, or go places where everyone drinks, the odds are that they won't stop drinking.

It's also true of the things you read and listen to. If you give this book to someone and they never read it, they will never understand how to change who they are to eventually find the love of their life.

I have a basic rule in my search for a partner. If she has not read and will not read *The Five Love Languages* by Gary Chapman, and follow those theories, I won't date her. That is how strongly I feel about understanding my partner and giving her what she needs to fill her love tank.

If your partner doesn't understand how to make you feel loved, how will you ever feel completely loved? If you don't understand how to fill your partner's love tank how will they ever feel completely loved? And, after all, according to Dr. Laura, the primary reason partners stray is because they are finding something in someone else that their partner is not offering.

All this means is, when your list is complete you will need to update it, change it, modify it, work with it until you truly find what makes you happy and then your job becomes how you will go about making your partner happy, too.

Know exactly what you are looking for. That means if you find it in a person, be ready to change your ideas and of course your "list" when you find that the thing you thought you wanted doesn't turn out to be exactly what you thought it would be.

EPILOGUE

Now let me ask again. What are you going to do differently now than you have done in the past? Are you going to the same places you have always gone? Are you looking for the same type of person you have always looked for? And have you evaluated what each item on your list will bring to the relationship?

I know there are going to be lots and lots of questions. Lots and lots of responses, arguments, disagreements with many of the things I have shared in this book but what is most important is this ...

Have you made your decisions, written them down, thought out what you want your next significant other to be like?

Have you opened yourself to change and becoming the most loving person you can become?

Have you decided that acceptance, understanding, compassion and communication are the only methods to finding and keeping the love of your life?

If you have, then I wish you a wonderful and amazing journey through many different areas in your life until you write to me and say, "Steve! I found the one! And we are wonderful."

Blessings, love and many hugs into your life.
~ Steve Sapato

steve@stevesapato.com
www.stevesapato.com

www.ingramcontent.com/pod-product-compliance
Lightning Source LLC
La Vergne TN
LVHW021540080426
835509LV00019B/2751